FOX TAILS

FOX TAILS
Nathan Cabot Hale

White Whale Press • New York

Acknowledgements

To my wife Alison B. Hale for her continuous encouragement, interest, and support.

To Walter Hearn for the design and typography of this book.

And to my friend of many years, Joan Lauri Poole, who is a poet of great sensitivity and an editor of skill and forbearance.

Library of Congress
Catalog Card Number:

Published by White Whale Press
Amenia, N.Y.

Printed and bound in the
United States of America

Books by Nathan Cabot Hale:

Welded Sculpture	1968
The Embrace of Life	1969
Abstraction in Art and Nature	1972
The Birth of a Family	1979
The Spirit of Man	1981

Contents

(Contents continued)

Introduction

If you want to know the origins and meanings of the poems in this book, you should understand that my work as a sculptor of the human figure is my source. My development of a welding technique for the figure enabled me to explore the expressions and movements of the human body in a new way. In creating figure compositions out of the fire of the sun, so to speak, I was led to reexamine the history and prehistory of human consciousness. Starting with the nude family, I have followed the figures through the races, the cultures and the religious beliefs of the world. During this time my efforts were always guided by the simple definition of the word "abstraction" . . . which means *to get to the root of* whatever is being studied. In my fifty years of studying the human figure, I have found that, no matter where it springs from, the figure contains common meanings that are sacred and holy. So these poems that I have written during the years of my work reflect in *words* the meanings that I have found in the *forms* of nature and the human spirit . . . things that I could not say in sculpture. This book is my legacy to you, and my wish for your fulfillment.

Nathan Cabot Hale
Amenia, N.Y. 1993

Reunion

Fox Tails

They wave in fields across the western hillsides . . .
In vacant lots or anywhere the land remains untouched . . .
They shimmer in the fair winds along the lower Sierras . . .
They are responsive to the slightest breeze . . .
These long-stemmed grasses we called fox tails.

Each year you see them spring forth from the earth . . .
Green as tender grass . . . but full grown by summer . . .
The children walk through fields of them . . . oblivious . . .
To the dart-like seed pods catching in their stockings.

A summer field of fox tails has a faint dry odor . . .
Something indefinably seed-like . . . coiled and waiting . . .
You pull the seeds off the stalk by running your hand . . .
Up the stem till the seeds are caught in your palm . . .
With a sharp continuity of motion you pull your hand . . .
And there they lie all clustered in a bunch like birds . . .
You can break them open and then . . . eat the tiny seeds.

I sat on the hillside of the Mount of Olives . . .
The place where Jesus walked with his disciples . . .
And watched the fox tails blow in the dry wind . . .
I saw back in time . . . could see the fox tails catching . . .
To the hem of his robes . . . as they do to everyone . . .
Even to the seams of his sandals . . . holding fast . . .
So that he carried them with him to the cross . . .
Alone . . . abandoned by his twelve followers.

We call them fox tails . . . they are the wild oats . . .
And they are fine . . . and fierce . . . and true.

≈

The Grove

A tall stand of eucalyptus trees ...
Borders the edge of the Sea of Galilee ...
At a place that was once a town ...
Now goatherds tend their flocks ...
And rest from the burning sun ...
In this grove on the western shore.

"I'm looking for Magdalla" ... I say ...
Hoping that they will understand ...
"Yes ... yes" ... they point to the earth ...
"Magdalla ... is here ... this place."

Confirmed that this is the site ...
I wander toward the waterside ...
Thinking of Mary Magdalen ...
The sainted woman ... the town whore ...
The loyal one ... the loving one ...
Tears come to my eyes ...
And I cannot tell why ...
Except for my knowledge of loyalty ...
So difficult to find in human souls.

I think she must have loved him ...
Far more than can be told ...
To follow as she did among the twelve ...
Knowing men ... as she did ...
Seeing daily proof of their hollowness ...
Wanting so to hug him to her breasts ...
Give him their softness and comfort ...
Following him even to Golgotha ...
Where they drove the nails ...
Into the flesh of his hands and feet ...
Wanting to hold him ... take the pain away.

I wandered back from the water . . .
Through the grove of eucalyptus . . .
The goatherds smile their friendliness . . .
"Magdalla" . . . they say . . . "this Magdalla."

≈

Reunion

You ask if we have met before . . .
Perhaps we have . . . my origins are complex . . .
But if you will sit with me awhile . . .
And share this minted tea . . . this summer afternoon . . .
We might find the reasons . . .
For our affinity.

I go back you know . . . beyond the present . . . a long road . . .
First . . . to hill country . . . with rocky limestone farms . . .
With a creek cutting through the land . . . meandering . . .
And a spring . . . richly pouring forth . . .
There are mysterious caves there too . . .
Leading deep under the ground . . .
To God knows where . . .
(One might settle for this . . . but it would be a mistake).

Farther back . . . an October sky . . .
A wooden ship with creaking spars . . .
Crossing an unknown sea . . . into the sun . . .
Do you have me yet?

No? . . . well before that . . .
A conglomeration of warring principalities . . .
And the always wandering urges . . . origins . . .
Sweating under various rulers . . .
Out of the old leveler's loins . . . Cromwell in fact . . .
But fighting with Plantagenet banners too . . .
Turmoil . . . back to the Roman and Greeks days . . .
But always finding the misty way . . .
Through Jerusalem . . . to Egypt . . .
It almost defies memory . . .
Yet I carry it with me . . .
The swimming upstream . . . the striving . . .

If pressed I might recall a building . . . a monument . . .
Or even a time . . . perhaps . . .
But seldom ever . . . a face.

As we sit here in the fading sunset . . .
Our tea now down to the bottom of the pitcher . . .
With only the smell of the mint remaining . . .
I find I can go even farther back . . .
To the animal days . . .
To that reign of terror and exhaltation . . .
But no . . . that is not yet it.

Now . . .
I think I see the sea once more . . .
The primordial sea . . .
The sea that first leapt toward the sun and moon . . .
The sea that broke new waves on fresh granite rock . . .
The sea that with the purest mother joy . . .
The smell of birth all around . . .
Gave forth the life . . .
Into the eastward moving earth.

Ah . . . that is it . . .
It is now that I know you . . .
And see you . . .
Swimming with me . . .
In your rapture . . .
Yes!

≈

The Coming of Light

Do not mourn . . .
The passing of the old myths . . .
The supernatural births . . .
The resurrections and ascensions . . .
The voices from on high . . .
Intoning admonitions.

These things come from . . .
The primitive past . . .
Were efforts . . .
To comprehend . . .
Vast complexities.

Now there are clearer truths . . .
Evolving . . .
From things at hand . . .
True miracles . . .
That unfold . . .
Before your eyes . . .
From the very substance . . .
Of life.

≈

Testament to Nature

I
Sacrament

Recognize . . .
That the body is . . .
The vessel of the soul . . . the spirit.

The soul and spirit . . .
Endure and continue . . .
Striving to perfect themselves . . .
In each new generation . . .
In transmigration and perpetuation . . .
Down all the years.

Our fragile bodies hold within . . .
The first life forms . . .
As well as . . . first man and woman . . .
They give their souls and spirits . . .
In the embrace of love . . .
Crossing all barriers of time and space . . .
Merging all . . . with God.

The energy within each body . . .
Pulses full of ecstasy . . .
But also with life's pain.

Desiring a less rigorous path . . .
We seek to ease the agony of evolution . . .
Protest . . . some times rebel against . . .
The very ways that lead us . . .
To the upright stance . . .
The shining forth of consciousness.   →

It is the sacrifice of egg and sperm ...
In perpetual loss ... in perpetual gain ...
That brings the sacrament of life ...
The closeness ... the truth ...
The immortality ...
Of soul and spirit.

II
Blood Sacrifice

She is the sister to the Moon . . .
Living in her pathway . . .
Keyed to her sequences . . .
Ebbing and flooding . . .
Like the rivers and the seas . . .
Coming into season . . .
At the fullness of her time . . .
Sacrificing the egg . . .
Giving up the blood . . .
In the perpetuation . . .
Of the species . . .
Of the kind.

Sister to the Moon . . .
and . . .
Mystery.

≈

III
Offering from the Earth

Some are smaller than a pinhead ... microscopic ...
Some as large as coconuts ... the seed of the palm ...
Others dry in pods that can be shaken like rattles ...
They blow through the air with filament sails ...
Catch in the fur of animals in transit ...
Are carried undigested in the bellies of deer ...
In the craws of birds of passage ...
Coming in sizes suitable to their species ...
Coming in numbers beyond telling.

Every wind bears seeds on its wings ...
Spreading fecundity to the continents ...
Rivers and oceans carry them afar ...
Each footfall presses in germinations ...
Grasses ... bushes ... trees ... and flowers too ...
The seedling gender of the earth.

These small and essential beings ... surrounded ...
Protected by nutrients ... sufficient to start life ...
The seasons ... expansion and contraction ...
Moisture ... do the rest.

There are the seedlings ...
Sprouting all around ...
Dancing toward the sunlight ... expanding ...
Sleeping in the contraction of night ...
Singing in God's own way ...
On many levels ...
With a richness ...
And sense of time ...
Far greater ... and more profuse ...
Than we can ever comprehend.

≈

IV
The Beginning

The Earth ... the foundation of life ...
Was here ... long before our kind appeared ...
Was here ... before the vertebrates were formed ...
Yes ... before the growing greenness of plants ...
The green that comforts rocks and plains ...
Softening all ... for our footfalls.

But something of us was here at the forming ...
Something of our spirit goes back to the beginning.
And through all the turns that life has made ...
Our spirit derives from the very dawn ...
From the formation of the sun and planets ...
For all were modeled ... all were formed ...
By the arms and hands of God ...
Shimmering in the blue-black night.

The earth arose from the swirling arms ...
Spinning and seething in their loving touch ...
Slowly accumulating mass ...
Slowly forming the magma core ...
The earth journeying around our days ...
The earth journeying around our years ...
Compounding the greatest journey of all ...
Around the galactic center ...
Held in the touch of love.

Then the eons of time when the crust was forming ...
To be broken up again in massive tectonic plates ...
Then thrust up again to form mountain ranges ...
Mountains that have lived and died ...
And have then lived again ...
Preparing for the coming of water ...
Preparing for the coming of plants ...
Preparing for the coming of life ...
Oh sing of the forming ... sing.

≈

V
We Are of the Water

We are of the water . . . creatures of the streaming . . .
The oceans . . . the surging seas . . . the rivers . . .
Moving endlessly across the earth . . .
Sending moisture upward to the sun . . .
Gathering in clouds . . . riding the air . . .
Forever forming . . . changing . . . softening . . .
Modeling the heart of the earth.

We are of the water . . . creatures of the rain . . .
The cleansing . . . washing . . . rain from above . . .
The falling mist that weighs the mountain branches . . .
Lying heavy on the pine boughs . . .
And dampening the mosses on the rocks . . .
Drenching the prairies and the plains . . .
Nourishing the springtime earth . . .
The rain that falls on the cities of men . . .
Cleansing them of sins . . . in time . . .
The rain that returns to the sea.

We are of the water . . . creatures of the ebb and flow . . .
Deriving our forms from its every movement . . .
Its tumbling . . . rollicking . . . plunge and splash . . .
Our joy is a spiraling jet of spray . . .
That leaps and dances down the stream's course . . .
Our somber moods come from the ocean deeps . . .
Where currents below currents move onward . . .
Sending waves rolling and breaking on distant shores.

We are of the water . . . creatures of the streaming . . .
We are of the water . . . creatures of the cleansing rain . . .
We are of the water . . . creatures of the ebb and flow . . .
Our waves roll and break on distant shores.

≈

VI
Emergence

Out of the reaches of the Cosmos ...
When in its path around the central sun ...
The spinning earth was formed ...
The sunlight flooded it with spirit ...
While from the heavens ... it drew the soul ...
And when the mountains and the plains ...
Thrust upward on the earth ...
The soul and spirit were given shadows of mood.

Then the mists came and the waters began to flow ...
Running in streams ... filling the great depressions ...
Forming lakes ... and seas ... and oceans ...
The streaming element covering the earth.

To the formed elements in rock and sand ...
Came the moisture ... came the softening ...
In its wetness ... in its changing seasons ...
Freezing and thawing ...
Alternating night and day ...
Expanding and contracting ...
In the soul of the Cosmos ... in the spirit of the sun.

From the life-infused seething earth ...
Came the urges for liberation ...
Animated by the flowing energy of the heavens ...
Entered into by the streaming formativeness of water ...
The first waves of life emerged ...
Pulsing within their membranes ...
Drawing to themselves and again releasing ...
The energy of the stars ...
The warmth of the sun ...   →

Each small creature . . . swimming . . . knowing itself . . .
Meeting with its fellows . . . rejoicing in life . . .
In the soul of the Cosmos . . . in the spirit of the sun . . .
The continuous . . .
Emergence.

≈

VII
The Cellular Self

The lens-shaped self ... all potential ... swimming free ...
Drawing its levels ... its movements of life ...
From the layered earth ... the layered atmosphere ...
Softened from the material state by the flow of water ...
Expanding within its tender membranes ...
Then releasing all again ...
Pulsing in continuous interchange ...
Returning to God.

All is possible within the living cell ... the one ... the many ...
The lens-shape drawing light ... focusing it within ...
Adjusting to gravity in swimming joy ... formed by it ...
Pulsing in response ... all nervous impulse ...
Drinking in the sea ... respiring ...
Tasting ... kissing ... everything in floating ambiance ...
Accumulating all within the self ...
Until the joyousness ...
In cosmic sharing ... divides ...
Becoming a second self.

Here ... in the layered body of the cell ...
The flow of movement ... the sense of being ...
Opens pathways ... radiations ...
Outward from this soul in all directions ...
This focus of creation ... this one-celled creature ...
This tiny universe touched by God ...
Filled with God ... and ready ...
To venture outward ...
Into the layered world.   →

And ready to venture inward . . .
Into its collected images . . .
From the earth's past . . .
Expanding its soul . . .
Its spirit . . .
In dreams.

≈

VIII
Radiating Outward–Spiraling Upward

From the self . . . leaps the soul to life . . .
Radiating outward . . . spiraling upward . . .
In search . . . in variation . . .
Through the mists of mood . . . evolving qualities . . .
Slowly making its way through myriad layers . . .
The inner world of form.

Through these doorways . . . all transpires . . .
Never ending . . . traveling the course . . .
Into the layers of the forms of the earth . . .
Into the layers of the forms of the atmosphere . . .
Animated by the endless flow of water.

Radiating outward . . . the cells group . . . reach . . . branch . . .
Playing changes of movement . . . of mode . . .
Some becoming like plants in their myriad forms . . .
Others like rocks along the streaming course . . .
Still others increasing their perception . . . until . . .
The revolution of the spinal column . . .
Brings new direction to the journey . . .
Allowing organs to group themselves . . .
According to their purposes . . .
Until the fish form fills the seas.

Spiraling upward . . . the first fish crawls up the beach . . .
Its pectoral fins stretching to become arms . . .
Its anal fins emerging into legs . . .
The gills becoming lungs . . .
In painful metamorphosis.   →

The final destination is within reach . . .
A few hundred million years away . . .
With arms outstretched . . .
Embracing all the earth . . .
God seems nearer . . .
To the mountains . . . to the heavens.

IX
We Carry Within Us

We have come great distances . . . up all the ages . . .
From that first venture up the beach . . . all is within us . . .
Out of our spinal column we have fashioned . . .
A head to house our eyes and thoughts . . .
Ribs to protect our breath and heart . . .
A pelvis to support our organs . . .
And protect our genitalia.

Though originally we stood on four limbs . . .
We have lifted up to heaven . . . balancing on two . . .
Altering the shape of our pelvis in the effort . . .
The shape of our rib cage too . . .
Now all is balanced on the frontal plane . . .
We look to the horizon . . . with changed perceptions . . .
Our organs and genitals face the world . . .
All senses radiating outward . . .
Following the cosmic forms.

Our stance says that we see . . . we hear . . .
We taste . . . we smell the odors on the wind . . .
We look into the heart of the world . . .
But more than that . . . our bodies say . . .
That we look upward . . . past the earth . . .
Past the present moment . . . past the trials of life . . .
Past the urgencies . . . past the annoyances . . .
That beset the life of every creature . . .
That we look to the heavens . . . to the spinning galaxy . . .
To see the face of God.

We carry all within us . . . the earth . . . the atmosphere . . .
The forming of the first cell . . . the shaping of the fish . . .
We all crawl up the beach of birth to breathe first breath . . .
Within us the evolutionary reaching of the ages . . . moves . . .
To touch his hand.

≈

X
Miracles

The sacred earth knows us . . . we are a part of creation . . .
We have wandered across continents . . . searching . . .
Searching for the truth without . . . for the truth within . . .
Sometimes lonely . . . sometimes desperate . . . sometimes dangerous . .
We have searched for the wondrous . . . the miraculous . . .
And finally have looked into our own bodies . . . our own hearts . . .
For the oldest . . . truest . . . miracles . . .
No wine to water . . . no loaves to fishes . . . no ascensions . . .
But rather . . . the true miracles of the soul and spirit.

In the embrace of the loving . . .
The circling of the sperm around the egg . . . its penetration . . .
The lighting of the spark of life . . . the beginning journey . . .
Up through evolution . . . perfecting the soul . . .
The limbs . . . the spinal column . . . budding . . . extending . . .
Surrounded by the love of the amniotic sea . . .
By the nurturing womb . . . and birth . . .
A series of miraculous events . . .
Complex beyond knowing.

The birth into life . . . awakening to love . . .
The searching spirit . . . questing . . .
Rising to the light . . . open-eyed . . .
The inherent wisdom awakening . . .
To the stratified earth . . . its layered atmosphere . . .
To the cosmic stream of weather.

We are the keepers of this earth . . .
We are the gardeners of the plants . . .
We are the guardians of the animals . . .
We are the protectors of miracles.

Let us be worthy.

≈

XI
The Knowing

To see beyond the moment . . . beyond personal advantage . . .
To perceive the truth . . . for the truth's sake . . .
Not as a defense . . . not as a weapon . . . not for gain . . .
But for the love of nature . . . for the love of God . . .
That is what knowing is . . .
And it is the last quality of life to evolve.

Our knowing emerges from our erect stance . . .
It is understanding nurtured by love . . .
It comes from basic sweetness and kindness . . .
It understands hurt . . . it understands melancholy . . .
But it expresses comfort . . . and feels joyousness . . .
It understands being with another's soul in oneness . . .
It comprehends betrayal . . . and the meanness of small people . . .
Because it has survived them . . . and never lost its love.

Knowing is the flooding of the heart at the sight of the surf . . .
The surging of the waves that rise on the sand . . .
It is the gull's cry . . . and the burrowing sand crab . . .
It is the kelp cast up on the shore after a storm . . .
It is the eternal salt smell of the ocean beach.

Knowing is the plain that stretches from the shore . . .
That undulates in its own waves all the way to the mountains . . .
It is walking on that plain in the summer's shimmering heat . . .
Seeing the startled quail rise in the hot afternoon . . .
It is the scent of cactus and of sagebrush . . .
Seeing another person in the far distance . . .
Wondering if that person is approaching . . .
Or leaving.

Knowing is the dispassionate acceptance of facts . . .
While being moved by them . . . but not upsetting the balance . . .

$\rightarrow$

Knowing stands at the foot of the mountain . . . looking upward . . .
It grows in the slow climb up the foothills . . .
In seeing a deer and its young . . . silently . . .
It is walking through the pine forest . . .
Through the ferns . . . listening for birds' songs . . .
It is reaching toward the mountain top . . .
It is resting on a crag and looking outward . . .
Seeing far . . . beyond ordinary vision . . .
And wondering at that . . . marveling.

Knowing is . . . above all things . . . coming home . . .
It is always the return . . . the bringing . . .
Of things found . . . impressions . . . pine cones . . . fish . . .
New friends . . . and the need for love and kindness.

Knowing is a way of being . . . living simple truth . . .
It loves the turn of a seashell . . .
The sprouting grain . . . a seedling tree . . .
The flight of a fledgling . . . a pelican's squawk . . .
The feeling of diving beneath a wave . . . and swimmimg out . . .
An infant's reaching in delight . . . its first steps . . .
It is the caring for the infant's health . . .
The desire to see it well . . .
And safe . . . within reason . . .
Until the time for venturing out . . .
Where all life must take its chances.

Knowing is the night that comes in darkness . . .
Making all obscure . . . hiding the familiar . . .
Making all a mystery again . . .
But opening up . . .
The splendor of the heavens.

≈

XII
The Faith of Life

The infant . . . child . . . the old . . . subsist on faith . . .
Though we may come to know the road in time . . .
The knowing cannot last . . .
The realm of trust spreads across the universe . . .
The heavens sing of being . . . and of faith.

The senses tell us of the earth . . .
At coming of age . . . in the years of maturity . . .
A segment of the Great Design . . . is revealed . . .
The lens-shaped cells see lighted earth and sky . . .
The breath inhales the motivating winds . . .
While fingers touch . . . and feel . . . the forming world . . .
The heart beats out the pulse of the spinning earth . . .
As we have come to know . . .
The evolution of our planet and our kind.

Our egos soared as we learned how our earth was made . . .
We came to comprehend our smattering bit . . .
We scoffed at faith and nurtured emptiness within . . .
And we played God in childish games . . .
Marching people up and down . . . slyly tricking our way . . .
Yet all occurred in the shadow-land of consciousness . . .
In the half-light reality of greed and gain . . .
Yet we will finally come around . . . to see the earth . . .
And we will see ourselves in full-dimensioned light . . .
Then we will take up the ultimate responsibility . . .
And base our knowing on our faith in life.

And we will stand on western shores . . .
And bid God-speed to the setting sun . . .
And we will welcome in the evening peace . . .
That slowly grows to darkness . . . and to sleep . . .
And with the faith of children . . . know . . .
That with the turning of the earth . . .
The sun will rise once more.

≈

Revelations

Birth

Utterly naked . . .
You arise from the sea . . .
The wetness of mother and father . . .
Falling from your body . . .
As the moonlight . . .
And the sunlight . . .
Draw forth your soul . . .
The shining newness of it . . .
Terrifying . . .
In its radiance . . .
Emerging.

≈

The Eyes

A reflected universe I see ...
Light collected by the lens ...
In a medium of water in a darkened pool ...
Blown in a breeze ... till wavelets ...
Catch and focus light ...
To the dark and retinal depths.

How intricate ... eyes ... yet simple ...
They are the windows to the world ...
We see the soul surround them ...
Respond with joy to make them dance ...
Or decline in pulled-back agony ...
Muddying the pool ...
Obscuring the bottom ...
With time-inflicted blindness.

They sweep the world in daily majesty ...
Surmounting all the rest ...
Faring forth to horizon and beyond ...
Gathering to themselves the light ...
From every nook and cranny of the world ...
Delighting in all ...
The facts of form that sally forth ...
Assessing with opinion each impression.

Oh yes ... the eyes reflect ... but they do more ...
They are of themselves ...
The purest essence of the universe ...
The crystals of the soul ... the life ...
Yet ... kin to puddles in the rain.

≈

Beyond the Wall

The barrier against the darkness . . .
Behind its defenses . . . lie . . .
Those ecumenical dreads . . .
Shared by all the world . . .
Waiting . . . in the inevitable future.

We sleep a troubled sleep . . .
Or lie awake for long . . .
To put up walls . . . to arm ourselves . . .
Concoct beliefs . . .
That almost always . . .
Make vast peoples march . . .
To standard or to hymn . . .
Sounding out with rote conviction . . .
Against that unknown . . .
That is feared . . .
As . . . unknowable.

Now men gather in cities . . .
As they have for millennia . . .
Creating meaningless events . . .
Harsh or poignant entertainments . . .
While they rob the future . . .
Of the earth . . . and . . .
Of themselves.

To see beyond . . .
Is not to fear.

≈

My Body Wakes

Storm tossed . . .
In the ocean of night . . .
Washed to the shore . . .
. . . of dawn . . .
My body wakes . . .
To the rising . . .
. . . of the sun . . .
The daylight . . .
Brings me consciousness . . .
. . . of the earth . . .
The singing.

Three Streams

Three flowing streams . . .
Distinct . . . yet intertwined . . .
Three streams defining . . .
The river of life . . .
Within.

The first . . . lifting . . .
With essences from far . . .
Savoring many worlds . . .
One current . . .
Just and kindly . . .
Raising to perception.

In its place . . . the second . . .
Smoothing and burnishing . . .
Dutifully caring . . . keeping . . .
All that is sustaining . . .
In bounds of love . . .
Flowing.

Upward from the earth . . .
The third rivering . . .
Losing and finding once again . . .
In desire . . .
The ultimate renewing.

Three streams defined . . .
Flow through the body . . .
Three . . . intertwining . . .
The river of life.

≈

Far Fetch*

Currents . . . the stirring life . . .
The deep fetch from out of slumber . . .
The far fetch . . . from . . .
Time beyond memory.

The currents cross . . . at . . .
Let us say . . . near sixty degrees . . .
Giving some chop . . .
Deflecting the ease of being . . .
That skirts the distant headland . . .
A rock strewn coast.

Out of the depths . . . the undercurrents . . .
The turbid boil of the living . . .
Night . . . in fevered shadow . . .
But worse in bright daylight . . .
The unsuspected . . .
Undertow.

The great spiraling currents . . .
Moving the seas . . .
The seasonal variation . . .
Of months . . . and years . . .
Bear onward . . .
Into time and futurity.

Onward . . . onward . . .
Through sunny days . . .
And star-enfolded nights . . .
While . . . somewhere . . .
Lightning strikes . . .
The distant seas.

≈

*Mariners refer to the distance between waves as the "fetch".

The Word

Illumination . . . from the far side . . .
The sound of speech . . . of song . . .
A voice inherent . . .
Speaking with trust . . .
With faithfulness.

A voice . . . that in silence . . .
We hear . . .
Singing songs . . .
Speaking.

I am a celebrant . . .
I am a hearer . . . listening . . . always . . .
Awaking to hear . . .
Sleeping to hear . . .
A celebrant sometimes worthy . . .
Sometimes not . . .
Waiting to receive . . .
The singing and the meaning.

From the intertwining spirals . . .
That meet in illumination . . .
Comes the singing . . .
The meaning . . .
Forming tones . . . colors . . .
Shaping . . . forming . . .
Worlds unending.

≈

Weavings

Attempting to reach outward . . .
Trying to understand . . .
I know that I repeat myself . . . that . . .
I am myself . . . a repetition . . .
Of the spiraling generation . . .
That spins the universe . . . and me.

It is called fate . . . or destiny . . .
A mysterious force . . .
That moves the hand . . . the eye . . .
Repetitive . . .
Over and over . . . it reproduces . . .
Beyond the surface film of knowing.

In interweaving lines of . . .
Shall I say . . . force . . . or energy . . .
(No matter)
This fatefulness . . . this destiny . . .
Calls out permutations . . .
Hopes of the future . . .
Cautions of the past . . .
That are conveyed . . .
In lightning turns . . .
Of accident.

Yet . . . in this spiraling generation . . .
The patterns endlessly unfold . . .

As from the pupate form . . .
The wings of fluttering life.

≈

Ardent Spirits

Yesterday ... it seems but yesterday ...
That I ... in the presence of nature ...
In the turbulence of seasons ...
Did try in vain to summon up ...
The spiritous past.

Today ... a distraction ...
I look away ...
And from the corner of my eye ...
On the edge of vision ...
It shimmers ...
That other world ... so full ...
Of implication.

My transitory consciousness ...
So vain and self-assured ...
Is thrown askew ...
Pulses ...
My body given over ...
To infinities.

Realities beyond ...
The glimmering awarenesses ...
That make the thing called ... I ...
Move in interstitial waves ...
Renewing me ...
To radiance ...
Once more.

≈

Bilateral Symmetry

An old woman ... her witching spells ...
Cast ... inward ...
An old woman ... encompassing ...
Surrounding all ...
Her will ... pervading ...
Enfolding darkness.

An ancient man opposing ...
Reaching outward ...
Striving upward ...
Along the seeming straightness ...
Of the spiral pathways ...
Spaceways ...
That lead to light.

These two ...
The two hands ...
The two legs ...
The two eyes ...
Seeking ...
Eternal balance.

≈

And Did I Once . . . And Did You?

And did I once?
And did you?
Surely . . . surely . . .
I did . . .
You did . . .
I mean press through . . .
From Eden . . .
In the ordeal of birth.

Oh . . . could I but remember . . .
And could you . . .
Those amniotic days . . . nights . . .
The blissful . . . surrounding sea . . .
A time of epochs . . . infinities.

I harken to the pulses . . .
The nerve sensations . . .
Yours and mine . . .
And seem to see . . .
Through hues of red . . .
Shades of vermilion . . .
That radiant universe . . .
Of triumphant convolution.

You . . . I know . . . have been . . .
In the realm of Gods . . .
Of cosmic formation . . .
Of purgatory . . . hell . . . and heaven . . .
In majestic confluence . . .

The pulsing here . . .
To me . . .
To you.

≈

The Stream

The snows melt . . . cascade downward . . .
Impelled toward the sea . . .
At the earth's center . . .
Could this be desire . . . this flowing . . .
This softening of stones and boulders?

I course downward . . . yearning over falls . . .
Into the whirl of pools . . .
The eddies of consciousness . . .
Streaming outward . . . beyond day and night . . .
Yet always assuming the undirected . . .
Meandering . . . way.

An ecstasy leads me . . .
To the run of the rapid's chaos . . .
I plummet . . . I swirl . . . I turn . . .
All sense of direction gone . . .
But the movement . . .
Plunging into all.

There . . . before me lies the calm . . .
The estuarial languor that is bliss . . .
In flowing filaments . . .
Her hair drifts by my face . . .
She is the sea . . .
At . . .
The earth's center.

≈

Or Not To Be

All that we really ever have . . .
Is the earth . . . and its seasons . . .
We have risen in yearning . . . and expectation . . .
Striving upward across the eons . . .
Arriving at last at the millennium . . .
The century . . . and the decade . . .
These have drawn us to . . .
The illusion of the urgent present.

In these times we have risen as individuals . . .
To marshal the yearnings . . . the expectations . . .
And all of the intimate desires . . .
Of children . . . youths . . . young women and men . . .
Of mothers with small children . . .
Of struggling fathers . . .
All of the ages with their dreams and urges . . .
And we have made trinkets and amusements of them . . .
We have made packages and coverings . . .
Of all the yearnings . . . all of the expectations . . .
And we have put them in the bazaar . . .
The marketplace . . .
The mall.

Yet all that we will ever have . . . is the earth . . .
The urgent present is our own invention . . .
We must learn to see again . . .
Across the eons and ages . . .
To become again . . . shepherds . . .
To become again . . . gardeners . . .
That we may see once more . . .
The earth pulsate with the seasons.

≈

To Love Is To Teach

Now is the time for the long haul . . .
For patience . . . for endurance . . .
It is not the time for intolerance . . .
It is the time to carefully explain . . .
And to explain again . . . and again . . .
It is the time to show what you are made of . . .
Your understanding . . . your humanity . . .
Your enduring warmth . . .
Your love.

You say that you are weary . . .
You say that you are heartbroken . . .
And this is . . . no doubt of it . . . true . . .
The lessons of life are hard won . . .
But people depend on you . . .
They draw their strength . . .
From your example . . .
You are the pivot of the world.

And because of this . . .
The world itself . . .
Draws its strength . . .
From what you are . . .
Not from what you feel at the moment . . .
But from what you are for all times . . .
From what you are . . .
For eternity.

≈

Dedication

To you,

To your mate,

and your children

The White Whale Press
RR 1, Box 5
Sheffield Road
Amenia, New York 12501

(914) 373-9380